ITALY

ANTIQUE AND MODERN GENIUS

WHITE STAR PUBLISHERS

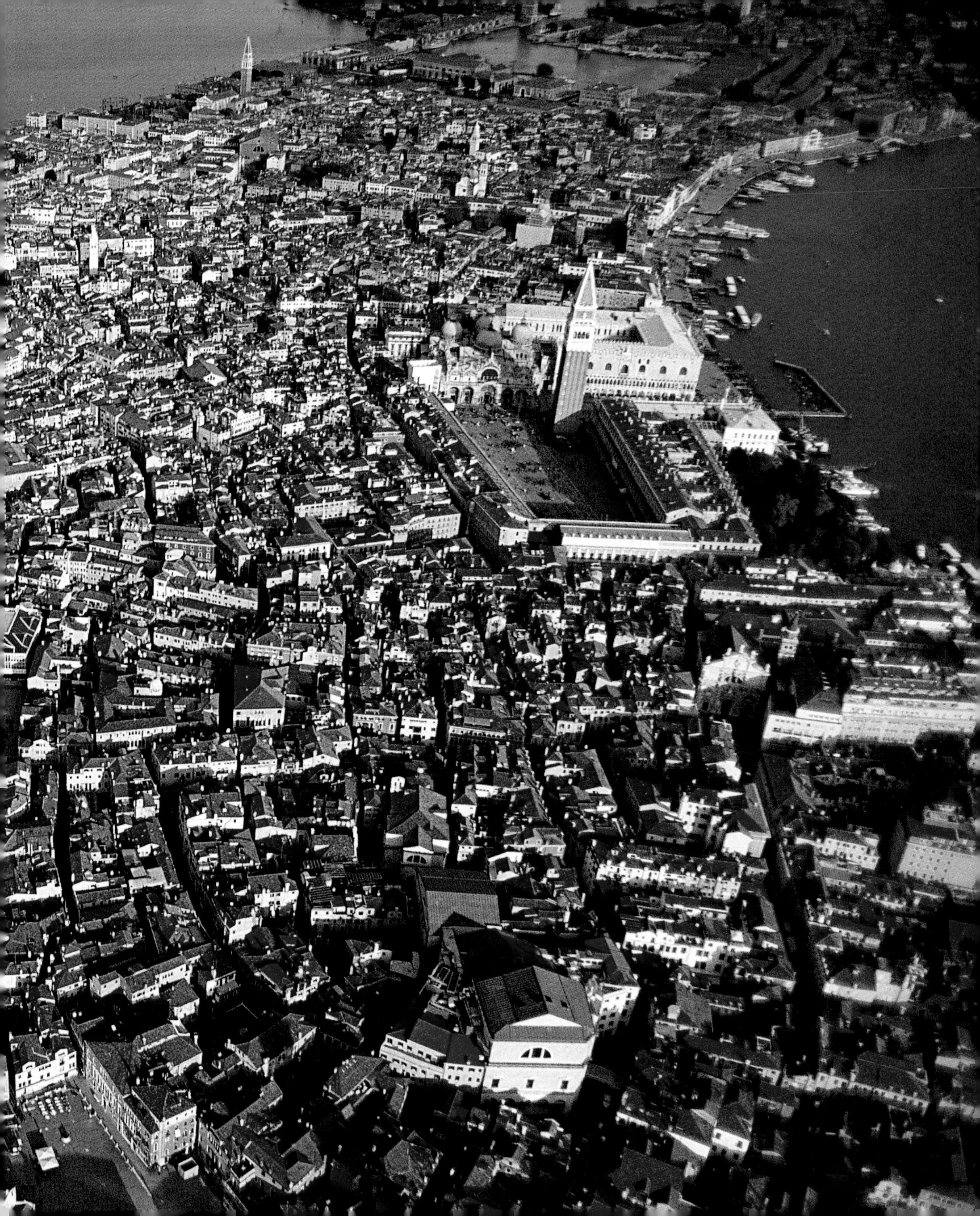

Text
Fabio Bourbon
Paola Aghini

Translation
Richard Reville

Graphic design
Patrizia Balocco

Contents

1 *The Milanese are very fond of the golden "Madonnina" that has watched over their city since 1700, when it was placed atop the central lantern. Bottom, Victor Emmanuel II exhorts his soldiers during the Battle of San Martino.*

2-3 *The venerable and magical city of Venice reveals its intricate network of winding* calli *and canals to those fortunate enough to be able to admire it from above.*

4-5 *La Scala is the pride of Milan and perhaps the most famous opera house in the world.*

6 *In the heart of Padua, the Piazza dei Signori and its magnificent monuments symbolize the city's former power.*

7 *Florence is dominated by the dome of the cathedral, also known as the Church of Santa Maria del Fiore. It is flanked by the Baptistery, left, and the Campanile, decorated by Giotto.*

8-9 *Rome shimmers in the central Italian sun, extending along the banks of the Tiber, the river on which the future "Eternal City" was founded.*

10-11 *This beach on Budelli Island, off Sardinia, is known for the warm pink color of its coralline sand.*

12-13 *Sunrise highlights the majesty of Cima Tosa, part of the Dolomite Range's Brenta group.*

14-15 *The medieval towers of San Gimignano loom over the town, bathed in the warm light of the setting sun.*

© 2006 White Star S.p.A.
New updated edition

© 1992 White Star S.p.A.
Via C. Sassone, 22/24
13100 Vercelli, Italy
www.whitestar.it

ISBN 88-544-0116-1

Reprints:
3 4 5 6   10 09 08 07 06

Color separation by Magenta Lit. Con., Singapore
Printed in Singapore

Introduction

In 1965, while orbiting the Earth high above Italy, the crew of Gemini 7 could clearly see that the country was shaped much like a boot. Defined by its position and peculiar shape, the Italian peninsula stands out as the most unusual geographical formation in Europe. Joined by Alpine mountains to the central regions of the old continent, the country reaches down to the very heart of the Mediterranean Sea, almost forming a bridge between Europe and Africa. By strange coincidence, and due to its pronounced elongation along a northwest-southeast axis, its extremities are equidistant in terms of both longitude and latitude.

Because of its location and physical features, Italy was the *caput mundi* of Roman civilization, a land much sought after by neighboring war-mongering populations. Later it was the cradle of the Renaissance of the Western world. It was the object of a revived nationalistic spirit during the mid-19th century. After being freed from two decades of dictatorship, it became the protagonist of an exceptional post-war economic boom. Italy now carries the image of an industrious nation in the avant-garde in the fields of technology and tourism.

The peninsula offers a variety of scenery, ranging from splendid mountains to barren, sun-drenched expanses where the only sound is the chirping of cicadas. Over and above its natural marvels, this land also offers the appeal of ancient civilizations and cultural movements that have animated it and made Italians so extraordinary lively and varied. It is precisely this heterogeneity that makes Italy so fascinating to the foreigner.

People have always identified Italy with pizza, macaroni and the mandolin. But cross the frontier, and it is easy to forget the things usually identified with Italy. To correct these preconceived ideas, begin your itinerary at Trieste, which famed poet Umberto Saba describes as having " a sullen grace. When it pleases, it is like a coarse, greedy youngster with blue eyes

and hands that are too big to present a lady with a flower; like a love affair tainted by jealousy..." This is the way the traveler sees its. The first impression is a rugged landscape typical of the Carso: grey rocks eroded by rain and hollowed out here and there by shallow *dolinas* perched along a stretch of sea from which the Vittoria righthouse emerges. This slender construction was built on the headland where an Austrian fort once blocked the road to Italy.

Here, the sea is both open and enclosed, merging on the horizon with the tip of the Istrian Peninsula and that of Friuli, where the Isonzo River flows to the Gulf. The symbol of the city, San Giusto's Cathedral, is harmonious due to the union of two parallel buildings dedicated to Our Lady of the Assumption and to the patron saint. The center of town life is Piazza Unità d'Italia, which opened at the end of the 19th century directly onto the sea. This monumental setting is surrounded on three sides by some of the most famous public and private buildings of the second half of the 19th century, such as the Town Hall and the headquarters of the Lloyd Triestino Insurance Company. The visitor who follows the merry comings and goings of the crowd that invades the square during the fine season and walks along the sea front enlivened by all types of quays and buildings will arrive at the Peschiera Pier, with its enormous fish market. By boarding a boat from the busy port, it is easy to reach Venice, a destination that has enchanted travelers of all times.

The visitor arriving by sea will enjoy the best view of this city, which seems to give itself generously but whose soul, in fact, is somewhat hidden. The emotion felt when landing in the *Serenissima*, admiring its monuments or walking through the tight maze of tiny streets and *calli*, is an immutable sensation even for those who know this town very well because the city always looks different, as if it were reborn each day with new verve and color. From the pier where the ships arrive, the visitor passes between two Byzantine columns surmounted by the statue of St. Theodore and the Lion of St. Mark, symbol of this ancient maritime republic. Beyond the Doge's Palace with its delicate stone lacework decoration is the shade of the majestic bell tower. From here the basilica fills the view; it is a magnificent Oriental dream which was built and decorated with the innumerable works of art brought from the East by sailing ships. The interior with its golden mosaics and soft light takes on added charm if seen while attending one of the classical music concerts periodically held there. Only then, without the hubbub of the tourists and filled only with intangible musical notes, does the visitors understand the true spirituality of the church.

16 With its Baroque garden containing a number of fountains and elegant statues, Palazzo Pfanner is doubtless one of the most charming patrician mansions in Lucca.

17 Palazzo Giusti in Verona has a splendid 18th-century Italian garden designed with mazes and long avenues of cypresses in accordance with the taste and style of the period.

18-19 The charming island of Isola Bella is an authentic treasure trove. Its famous terraces were built by Count Carlo Borromeo for his wife Isabella they lived in the 16th century.

Venice does not end in St. Mark's Square. On foot or by gondola, and never with haste, the visitor only has to proceed into any of its *calli* to come across historic buildings full of art treasures or a bar that has hosted famous names of the past. If, however, a visitor tires of monuments and churches and wants an alternative, he or she can also find pleasure in visiting Venice's most secret corners or relaxing in the sun in a little square before continuing the tour to Punta della Dogana, where a visit to the church of the Madonna della Salute is a must. Here, in the shady sacristy, the eyes of the guests in Tintoretto's well-known painting of *The Wedding at Cana* seem to follow those of the observer. An evocative atmosphere can be felt everywhere, and this explains how the Regata Storica and the fancy-dress Carnival can become unique spectacles. The latter is perhaps the only event in which Venetians mix willingly with tourists.

Although it is not far away, Padua offers quite a contrast to Venice. Of all the cities in the Veneto region, it has perhaps the least monumental appearance, although it abounds in valuable works of art. The Cappella degli Scrovegni has a famous cycle of paintings by Giotto, quite distinct from the works the artist did in Assisi because of their deeper lyricism and more careful depiction of the psychology of his subjects. Not far from here are the vegetable and flower stalls of Piazza delle Erbe. Overlooking this square, Palazzo della Ragione contains a colossal wooden statue of a horse made at the end of the fifteenth century for a tournament that took place in the Piazza dei Signori. The nearby university is the second oldest in Italy, and it was here that Galileo taught mathematics and dramatist Goldoni took his law degree. In the neighborhood, Pedrocchi's is a favorite haunt of local intellectuals—it was also once the scene of conspiracies during the Austrian occupation. St. Anthony's Basilica is the spiritual fulcrum of a city in which Eastern elements provide a contrast to the Romanesque and Gothic lines which are clearly of Western inspiration.

Another city with much to offer from an artistic and cultural point of view is Verona, world renowned as the setting for the love story between Romeo and Juliet. During the summer months, an open-air representation of this famous tragedy can be seen in the Roman Theater. At the same time of year, visitors can listen to an opera in the spectacular setting of the Arena. A strange legend has it that the imposing amphitheater was nearly completed in a single night by the Devil himself, as he had made a pact with a wealthy local squire who had been sentenced to death for committing a serious crime. As the squire pleaded desperately for mercy, he was told that if he could build an enormous edifice between the Ave Maria of the evening prayers and the following morning, his life would be saved. He had no other choice but to exchange his soul for the Devil's help. An army of demons worked all night long and the building was almost finished when the fatal hour struck. The demons returned to Hell and the Arena remained incomplete; it is easy to imagine

what happened to the heartless squire. The monument remains one of the best preserved masterpieces of Roman engineering in the world, despite the fact that it was seriously ravaged during the Middle Ages. Of a decidedly 14th-century flavor, the magnificent Piazza delle Erbe is filled with the awnings of market stalls. Going on to the nearby Piazza Dante, it is well worth looking up at the Arco della Costa, which has taken its unusual name from a whale's rib that whitens as it hangs under the large supporting arch. The entire center of Verona is a maze of tiny streets and historic mansions. The city also boasts an excellent cuisine which includes some of the traditional dishes of the Veneto region such as *paperete*, a type of pasta, chicken livers, and the renowned *frittura*, a mixture of fried fish. Last but not least,

there is the famous Pandoro cake. After satisfying the palate, the walking tour can be continued by going along the Adige, passing by the Cathedral and the superb Castelvecchio, to finally arrive in front of the splendid Romanesque basilica dedicated to St. Zeno, the city's patron saint. A visit, here is not to be missed, as one of the most important paintings of the Italian Renaissance, a triptych by Mantegna, is on the high altar of this church. Mantua, located in Lombard territory though linked to the Veneto by spirit and culture, owes its unusual aspect to the course of the Mincio River, which enlarges like a lake to surround it on three sides and gives it the aspect of a lagoon. Nearby marshes and swamps are populated by thousands of wild ducks, coots, herons, and egrets: it is not at all surprising that this natural environment becomes a paradise for bird watchers from spring to late summer. Because of its natural isolation, Mantua has been able to keep its original medieval appearance as a city of art and culture. It was in the central Piazza Sordello that in 1349 Petrarch received the laurel crown that made him poet laureate. The Castello di San Giorgio and the Palazzo del Te are visually stimulating constructions of undoubted charm, and the ducal palace of the Gonzaga family ranks second only to the Vatican as one of the largest monumental complexes in Italy. A little farther south, arriving in the rich, green countryside of Emilia, it is impossible to resist the call of Ferrara, whose magic dates from the Renaissance, though it still has the traces of its medieval civilization.

Here, humanity left one of its most significant traces. The ground echoes with history. The monuments seem to reawaken the ghosts of the noble ladies and knights of whom Ariosto sang. Among the Renaissance arts encouraged by Gonzaga dynasty, the cuisine should not be forgotten. Ferrara is highly renowned for the eels of the nearby delta; another typical dish is *salama da sugo*, recalled by Bacchelli in his novel *Mulino del Po*.

After one crosses the valley of Comacchio, the city of Ravenna soon becomes visible on the horizon. Today Ravenna is a few miles from the sea, but originally it was a small island at the mouth of Po, as shown by the mausoleum of the ruler Theodoric. This city is famous for the superb mosaics which adorn the interior of monuments such as the Basilica of San Vitale, forming such a contrast with the simple, almost austere exteriors. The mortal remains of Dante are in Ravenna in a modest, somewhat disappointing building, given the image the Italians have of this great poet.

Leaving behind the poignant architecture of Ravenna, the visitor arrives at the popular beaches of Romagna, as famous for its seaside resorts as for the hospitality of its people and the worldliness of its numerous meeting places. From Milano Marittima to Pesaro, the coast is packed with villages and towns that are busy until dawn with a frenzied nightlife enjoyed by tourists and the young people who flock to its many futuristic discothèques. A bit inland, the scenic medieval village of Gradara is situated on a hill and still protected by ancient walls. This tiny center is dominated by the huge castle in whose rooms the tragic love between Paolo and Francesca da Rimini developed. Lining the steep, narrow streets are craft workshops and food shops featuring *piadina*, a sandwich made with two slices of flat, unleavened bread, a delicious specialty claimed both by the Marches and Romagna regions.

In the hills of the Marches, travelers have the opportunity to admire the highest expressions of Renaissance architecture in the town of Urbino, an almost perfectly preserved jewel dating from the 15th century. In summer, this usually quiet town is enlivened by exciting cultural, artistic and social events which show it in all its splendor. There is still a strong attachment to the medieval past in this region, and the large number of pageants bears witness to this. A celebration that recalls former wild boar hunts takes place at Mondavio between the valleys of Metauro and Cesano, and another, the "Tornero della Quintana," takes place annually at Ascoli Piceno.

Now Umbria comes into view, a region rich in history and unique for its generous scenery.

20 *The marvelous park designed by Luigi Vanvitelli for the Royal Palace at Caserta stretches for nearly a mile with spectacular effect, incorporating pools, fountains and artificial waterfalls.*

21 top *A group of statues representing the myth of Actaeon decorates one side of the Grande Cascata, or Great Waterfall, in the gardens of the Royal Palace at Caserta.*

21 bottom *Built on the orders of the Bourbon King Charles III (1716-1788), the Royal Palace at Caserta soon became known as the "Italian Versailles" because of its massive scale and grand perspectives.*

22 top *St. Mark's Basilica is the pride of Venice. Above the doorways, semicircular lunettes frame colorful mosaics in intricate moldings.*

22 center *The Doge's Palace, magnificent residence of the Venetian rulers, is a testament to the power and splendor of the old Venetian Republic.*

22 bottom *St. Andrea's Basilica is the main monument in the city of Vercelli and one of the earliest examples of Gothic architecture in Italy.*

23 *With a solemn, three-naved interior and a polygonal cupola, Parma Cathedral is one of the best surviving examples of Italian Romanesque architecture.*

Its spiritual capital is without doubt Assisi, and its basilica is dedicated to St. Francis. This is truly the heritage of the whole of humanity, built with generous donations sent from throughout the Christian world. The church is subdivided into two parts. The saint's tomb is in the Lower Church, framed by frescoes painted by Cimabue, while the Upper Church is renowned for the 28 frescoes which Giotto painted to illustrate the life of St. Francis. The serious damage inflicted by the earthquake that struck Umbria in 1997 has been repaired by extraordinary and extremely delicate restoration work in the Upper Church, completed in 2005, and in the monastery, only commenced in 2006. The small medieval houses, the numerous holy buildings, the noble mansions, and the craftsmen's workshops seen along the way render even more precious the mystical setting of these structures. Nearby is the small town of Deruta, world renowned for the production of artistic ceramics, which flourished notably in the 16th century. In Foligno in September, it is well worthwhile to see the renowned Quintana tournament. During this exhibition, men galloping on horseback at a furious pace try to remove with their lances the ring that hangs from the arm of a wooden statue of a Moor in the center of the arena.

Crossing the Abruzzo region, whose magnificent natural beauty reaches its high point in the Abruzzo National Park, it is still possible to see the brown marsican bear in its natural habitat. At this point, the Adriatic coast is close, at the point where the headland of Gargano juts out into the sea. Green, gnarled Aleppo pines grow on the steep white cliffs that rise from the sea, hiding the little pebbly beaches that can often be reached only by water. The people here speak such a broad dialect that other inhabitants of this region describe someone who speaks in an incomprehensible way by saying that he is a *giargianese*, or a person from Gargano.

The Tremiti Islands, whose steep coasts are surrounded by an eternally blue sea, can be seen from these golden sandy beaches. Proceeding along this splendid coast, perhaps stopping off at Manfredonia to enjoy a tasty dish of spaghetti with mussels and other seafood specialties, the visitor soon reaches Bari, one of the most active towns of the Apulian region. Without doubt the most interesting part is the old section of the town in which rises the Basilica of San Nicola. Its austere façade makes it one of the most majestic churches in southern Italy.

An unforgettable route continues down to Taranto via Castellana, renowned for the mysterious caves discovered there in 1938. Then comes Alberobello, a small village with characteristic, cone-shaped houses known as *trulli* before finally arriving in sunny Locorotondo, where parching thirst can be quenched with a glass of good local wine. Like Bari, Taranto is divided into two distinct zones.

There is an old part, a tiny, charming islet surrounded on the opposite bank by a more modern zone. In these districts some streets are so narrow that only two people can walk along them side by side: the narrow paths were a form of defense from the periodical Moorish invasions. In the fishermen's quarter there are many stalls where passers-by can buy freshly caught seafood. The lucky and patient can see the ceremony in which the ships of the Italian Navy enter the so-called Mar Piccolo (the Small Sea) by way of the swing-bridge which links the old and the new parts of the city. On the route are beautiful beaches that face the Gulf and soak up the hot sun. For people who like rugged walks, this area, especially where it borders on Basilicata, offers interesting walks across the Murge, calcareous mountains and gullies hollowed out by rainwater. Remains of ancient homes, caves and churches dug out of stone in the Middle Ages are hidden between these gullies. An almost intact example of these successive developments undergone by these dwellings can be found in the Sassi di Matera.

Here it is interesting to climb up the steep, narrow streets and go into the houses or the local shops. In this archaic setting, classic films such as *The She-Wolf* (Alberto Lattuada, 1952) and *Christ stopped at Eboli* (Francesco Rosi, 1979) were made. This rugged and undulating scenery continues into the region of Calabria, a land of great contrasts, with green pine trees covering the Sila mountains and typical Mediterranean vegetation on the coast. Near Catanzaro there are still communities which hand down from father to son the traditions and language of their Albanese forefathers who arrived in 15th century the period of Aragonese rule. On clear days, both seas can be seen from high points, and in ancient times there was a great deal of commercial traffic on these waters. This area has always been plagued by strong winds and surging sea currents; these gave rise to the myth of Scylla and Charybdis, the terrible sea monsters that were supposedly responsible for so many shipwrecks in ancient times. In recent years spectacular archeological finds have been made, now exhibited alongside the famous Riace Bronzes fished out by the sea in 1972, and kept in Reggio Calabria. With modern navigation techniques, crossing the straits is no longer a problem. Indeed, it is worth taking a ferry to enjoy the magnificent view one has approaching this island that, according to Homer, was inhabited by Cyclops. This region is mainly mountainous, and its highest point is the massive Etna volcano. The best view of this mountain is from Taormina and from the ruins of the great Greco-Roman theater for which Etna provides a permanent backdrop. On this historical stage, the tragedies of the great Greek

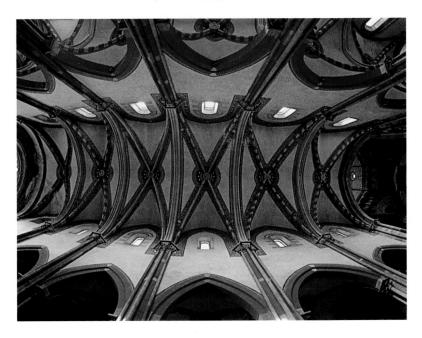

dramatists are still played, sometimes in the original language, and made even more intense by the marvelous scenery. Between these parched horizons it becomes clear that Sicily's greatest attractions are living history and its uncountable monuments that bear witness to the continuous presence of invaders.

Palermo is an impressive city because of the architectural styles left by the Phoenicians, Greeks, Carthaginians, Romans, Normans, French and finally by the Spanish. Piazza dei Quattro Canti, surrounded by the façades of beautiful Baroque mansions, is a very good starting point from which to begin a walk around the city. From here, it is easy to get to the sumptuous cathedral, which was begun in the 12th century and which contains the tombs of the Norman kings in an almost fairy-tale setting. The Cappella Palatina is another treasure chest which sums up the highest expression of three civilizations: Byzantine, Arab and Norman. A walk around the center, which is dotted with palm trees and exotic plants, will lead to Arab domes or the Baroque forms of tumbledown mansions, all of which help explain, the chaotic spirit and soul of the Sicilian people.

A ferry trip from the busy port of Palermo brings us to Sardinia, Italy's other big island, which has a very particular history of its own. This mountainous island offers some of the most spectacular beautiful scenery in the entire country. Its morphology ruggedly highlights the differences between the plains, the mountains and the plateaus where there are few villages and where the island's most ancient soul resides. Even the coasts, despite an illusion of uniformity, have a great variety of shapes, and many beaches, coves and spectacular rock formations alternate with each to form the most evocative of natural landscapes. The transparent emerald-green water and the distinctive pink sands are a permanent invitation to do nothing but enjoy life. In the interior, the historical and artistic heritage of this region is different from that of any part of the nation. No one can ignore the presence of the *nuraghi*, the megalithic, cone-shaped constructions built with enormous stones, or the presence of the even more mysterious *Domus de Janas*, small rooms without windows which were dug out of the rock and which have fostered the belief that, in ancient times, Sardinia was inhabited by gnomes. The old part of the island's capital, Cagliari, is built on a high hill dominated by the castle and towers. Around this the more modern quarters have been built, descending gradually toward the sea and the wharves where the intense activity that characterizes the biggest port of this part of Mediterranean is carried on. Opening out onto this busy stretch of water is the wide and elegant

24 *One of the most famous towers in the world for the elegance of its proportions and uniqueness of its tilt, the Leaning Tower of Pisa was the testing ground for Galileo's famous experiments on falling objects. Over the centuries the tower's tilt increased to the point that work to "straighten" the tower became essential. This was successfully completed in 2001.*

25 top *Visible from al parts of the city, the massive Lanterna, or lighthouse, at the end of the Vecchio Porto has become the symbol of Genoa.*

25 bottom *The medieval towers of Bologna are a source of pride for the capital of the Emilia region. Though not famous as the Tower of Pisa, some of these towers also lean.*

Via Roma, marking the center of the town, and filled at dusk with relaxed strollers. Roads go off from here and climb gently the hill, and this is where one can admire precious and solemn traces of the past that have remained intact despite the city's extensive development.

Heading back to "the continent," (Sardinians always call Italy *il continente*) by air or by sea, the visitor now reaches Naples. Arriving by sea, and after passing the Isle of Capri, one can catch a distant glimpse of the lovely island of Ischia. Then the city of Naples comes into view with its houses built in terraces on the surrounding hills. Everything is dominated by the threatening form of Vesuvius. For many people, this chaotic and vital city represent the unruly side of Italy. The sun, the tarantella and the philosophy of living day by day have always been considered, perhaps rightly, to sum up the people of Naples. Everyday life can be observed by exploring the busy streets in the old part of the city where confusion reigns, where entire families live in so-called *bassi*, small, narrow rooms on the ground level, and where most of the daily work is carried out in the streets. It is this exuberance that gives Naples its charm, as do its street festivals and popular traditions including the famous Neapolitan song festival, founded in honor of the Madonna di Piedigrotta, or the celebration of the miracle of the liquefaction of San Gennaro's blood. San Gennaro is the city's patron saint, and it is said that the luck of the city for the following year depends on this miracle. (It is considered to be a bad sign if the blood does not liquefy.)

Numerous monuments bear witness to a glorious past and also keep alive memories of the city's history. The imposing Maschio Angioino still seems to protect the entrance to the port, whereas in the Cappella Sansevero the two statues of Disinganno and Pudicizia (Disenchantment and Modesty) continue to amaze viewers with their unparalleled technical virtuosity. This building holds many legends, all as mysterious as the patrician who, in the 18th century, built it as his tomb. One could say that there is a particular myth linked to every corner of Naples. In addition to all the other claims the city can make, it also known as the unrivaled queen of the pizza. This popular dish is prepared in many different forms, ranging from the classic round to the *pizza a metro* (by the meter) which one can buy in slices.

From the summit of Vesuvius, there is a fine view of the plain that was once the site of Pompeii and Herculaneum, the two Roman cities buried by the eruption in A.D. 79. Archeological excavations, which have lasted more than a century, have provided a conception of daily life almost 2000 years ago. There are other surprises to be discovered along the Amalfi coast, the superb, natural paradise along which precipices and vertiginous cliffs open onto a crystal-clear sea. The area of Circeo to the north is also renowned for its beaches and the pretty seaside villages that compete with each other for wonderful scenery. Ever since the days of the Roman Empire, the entire area, as far as Fregene and beyond, has been a favorite spot for spending the summer months.

Today this coast is still crowded with inhabitants of Rome, who, in their free time, prefer to flee the chaotic metropolis in which they live. Despite the easy-going mentality of these people, Rome is a city in continual movement, partly because of the thousands of tourists who invade it every day. It is amazing to see how the traffic manages to get around the innumerable vestiges of the past, from the Colosseum to Piazza Venezia, from Castel Sant'Angelo to Trinità dei Monti, with such nonchalance. Romans still take pride in the traditions of Rome as *caput mundi*. Their pride is fully justified by the magnificence of this city. Walking through the Imperial Forums, the visitor is reminded of the ancient pomp. Along the narrow streets of Trastevere, it is easy to forget that this is in the capital; this area gives the impression of being in a small village of old Latium, with children playing ball and gossip chatting at the window. In the center between Piazza Navona and the Trevi Fountain, there are some very quiet streets onto which face picturesque restaurants offering wine from the Castelli Romani, or the lesser known *fragolino* wine. Observing the famous Bocca della Verità, the Roman mask that, according to tradition, bites off the hand of anyone who tells a lie, it is strange to think that Rome is the bureaucratic city par excellence, heart of the animated and often contradictory political life of the country. Equally important decisions are made in the heart of the Eternal City, in the tiny but extremely powerful Vatican State, the seat of the Pontiff. St. Peter's Basilica, surmounted by Michelangelo's dome, is the symbol of Christianity, and the nearby Vatican Museums contain some of the world's greatest cultural treasures.

Siena is a close relation to Rome, at least according to a legend that says it was founded by Senius, the son of Remus, brother of Romulus. This city has great charm and is very pleasant to tour on foot, especially during the colorful and exciting Palio, a horse race run on July 2nd and August 16th every year. The entire city lets itself go with uncontrollable merrymaking that involves each of its 17 districts. The exciting horse race takes places after a sumptuous procession in which

26-27 *Masterpieces of Greek sculpture dating from the 5th century B.C., the bronze statues of Riace spent more than 2000 years at the bottom of the Ionic Sea before they were discovered accidentally by a fisherman in 1972. It is thought that these two enormous bronze statues of warriors were lost during a storm on a voyage between Calabria and Greece. They are now the principal attraction in the Museo Nazionale della Magna Grecia in Reggio di Calabria.*

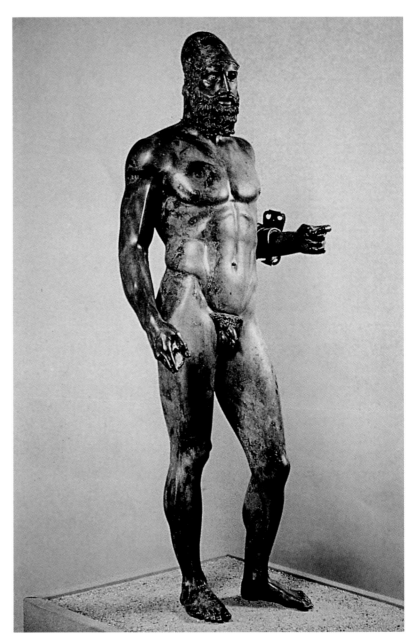

Renaissance costumes and a performance by the famous flag wavers vie for applause.

Florence, too, has it own charm, due to medieval and Renaissance architecture within the old walls which give a proud and elegant character to the city. The inhabitants are austere and critical, but can also be brilliant; they possess a pungent wit. The historical center between the Cathedral, the Palazzo Vecchio and the Palazzo Strozzi is still the throbbing heart of city life, heightened by a cosmopolitan crowd. The shops in Via Calzaiuoli, Via Roma and Via Tornabuoni are the most elegant and exclusive, as are the numerous meeting places located there. The glittering shop windows are in strong contrast with the nearby Mercato della Paglia, home to all sorts of curiosities - including objects made with the famous red Florentine leather, and in May, tiny cages containing chirping grasshoppers. From the panoramic Piazzale Michelangelo, the view extends beyond Brunelleschi's cupola and Giotto's campanile to embrace the rolling hills that surround the city. Florence has managed to conserve many green areas close to the city center.

Passing fields divided by rows of cypresses in the countryside around Fiesole and proceeding through the Tusco-Emilian Apennine forests, we reach the Po plain, which is announced by the opulent city of Bologna. This city is universally known as *la dotta* (cultured) and *la grassa* (fat). The first of these nicknames is due to its long cultural tradition; it was here at the beginning of the 13th century that Europe's oldest university was founded. The second nickname is derived from the worldwide fame of the local gastronomy. Tortellini, tagliatelle, suckling pig and good wine explain why it is common to think of Bolognese woman as being beautiful and glowing with health. From the tops of its towers, of which the Asinelli and Garisenda are the most famous, the visitor can enjoy a panorama enhanced by the city's red roofs. A walk through the arcades of this regional capital helps explain the Bolognese spirit and the openness and hospitality of its people.

Unlike Bologna, Genoa appears prouder and more closed, almost as if its inhabitants still felt the need to fight for independence; or perhaps this is due to the fact that this city is not only Italy's the biggest but also a large industrial center. Despites its fame as a commercial town, Genoa is above all a beautiful city. Because of the majestic way in which the buildings rise from the seafront and the haughtiness of its monuments, it is known as *La Superba*, or *The Proud*. Its beauty lies in the contrast between old and new: in streets that have a quiet, aristocratic air about them, in the tangle of *caruggi* (lanes) full of confusion and

28-29 28 and 29 *The island of Burano, in the Venice Lagoon, is studded with the characteristic multicolored façades of fishermen's houses. The handsome campanile of the Church of San Michele, built in the typical style of the Lagoon, can be seen in the background, on the left.*

30-31 *Elegance and beauty parade the streets of Milan, the Italian capital of style. The smoky industrial city of the Fifties, Sixties and Seventies has now almost completely disappeared and the haute couture market has become an important component of the thriving new local economy.*

agitation, and in the glimpses of the panorama that can be caught of the hinterland or the seaside.

The fact that tasty *pesto* was invented here as well as many other delicacies may hide the fact that the Genoese are known for their avarice. However, the fact that their region principally consists of an arch of mountain and steep hills, and their only resources come from a narrow strip of arable land and from the sea; which is a situation that may help to justify this reputation.

Ligurian scenery is varied, as is that of the entire territory of the region. Genoa is in the center of the arc: to the east in the Riviera di Levante, inaccessible because of its rocky, high, steep coasts with small, deep inlets and coves enclosed between narrow headlands. The villages that give the name Cinque Terre to the area seem to have been wedged by force between the cliffs and the sea, and have kept a good deal of their old charm. There are tiny creeks and coves on the headland of Portofino where the sea, rocks, greenery, and animal life are wonderful to see. To the west of Genoa is the Riviera di Ponente, also called the Riviera dei Fiori because of the cultivation of flowers on the hills overlooking the sea. This coast is less harsh, with gentler reliefs and shallower inlets where sandy beaches form one of the world's best-knows tourist attractions.

Beyond the Northern Apenines, the much richer land of Piedmont in the zones known as Langhe, Asti, and Monferrato is famous for the beauty of its scenery and even more so for its excellent wines. This is the more intimate, secluded Piedmont that even people who live in the same region do not know. Here each tiny village has its own history, with clues provided by the presence of numerous castles or the votive pictures in the numerous chapels in the country.

Leaving these magnificent hills and following in the footsteps of the many people who have preferred to abandon hard work in the fields, one arrives in Turin, an elegant and slightly old-fashioned city. *Piedmontese falso e cortese*, "false but polite" says the proverb, and it is perhaps true. Turin is symbolic of this region and presents itself as a distinguished, refined, and snobbish city. Toward the outskirts it is possible to see the signs of the formidable economic power developed by heavy industry during the past century. However, the reverberations of the economic boom of the Sixties and Seventies had ceased by the end of the Seventies, and Turin was forced to create a new identity, no longer fully linked to industry, but dedicated to the so-called "advanced services sector," constituted by services,

banks, research centers, etc. Following bleak years of adjustment, the city embarked on a series of ongoing redevelopment projects and is now an important magnet for cultural activities of all kinds, from literature and research to fashion and music. Furthermore, its prestigious designation as the venue of the 2006 Winter Olympics has finally allowed the austere Piedmontese capital to secure a new international role.

Turin can boast a unique urban layout with straight, three-lined boulevards and vast scenic settings such as that of Piazza San Carlo, which everyone considers to be the city's salon. Of the many museums the most important is the Egyptian Museum, second in size only to the one in Cairo. The records of the long battle for Italian unity can be added to the city's already remarkable cultural attractions. Quite visible from the top of the Mole Antonelliana or the Superga hill, the Val d'Aosta opens on the horizon, with the unmistakable form of the Serra of Ivrea, an immense glacial moraine formed in prehistoric times, in the foreground.

In the midst of Europe's highest mountains, among which the imposing massif of Mont Blanc stands out, the Valle d'Aosta is dominated by the immense expanse of Monte Rosa, a gigantic stone sentinel which forms the border with Switzerland. It is indeed a unique spectacle. The Alpine panorama is characterized by the jagged contours of the highest peaks and the imposing walls

of granite whose dominating colors range from the grey to the white of the eternal snow, softened in summer by the intense green of the pine forests.

The Gran Paradiso National Park, situated in this spectacular area, is the largest and most important in Italy. Here it is possible to see ibex and chamois climbing up the steep paths and the grassy slopes of the mountain. There is a very strong "francophone" tradition in this region, easily recognized from the dialect and local place names.

The area is dotted with numerous manors overlooking the road that leads to Aosta, a town that was founded by Julius Caesar's legionaries and that is among the best preserved of the Roman Empire. Many of the villages nestled in the valley have been transformed into well-equipped skiing resorts in the last 30 years, and they attract crowds in all seasons because of their wonderful scenery and folklore traditions.

Among the many valleys, each one leading to a spectacular group of mountains, the Valtournanche has the Matterhorn, second only to the majestic Mont Blanc. The harsh grey of these granite massifs, covered with permanent glaciers, is completely different from the warm rosy shade of Dolomitic limestone which is the fortune and glory of the Cime di Lavaredo, which with other peaks at the eastern end of the Alpine arc, is a major attraction for mountaineers.

The Dolomites have their own unmistakable personality: there are no two peaks equal in shape, appearance, or legend, or that present the same consistency to the climber's hand. Massive towers with sheer walls, minutely indented crests, and sharply pointed mountain crests rise from the vast meadows at their base. The rocks, join up generally of a reddish color, take on pink, red, and violet hues at dawn and dusk. They shine on from high when the valleys are in the shade, and make the Dolomites one of the most popular destination for international tourism. With spectacular peaks, large coniferous woods; and small blue lakes framed by dark forests, this region is ideal for holidays, winter sports, and mountaineering.

Many tourist centers, including as Cortina d'Ampezzo, Merano, Ortisei, and Pieve di Cadore, are favorite destinations for the Milanese who, after a long week spent amid the skyscrapers of the city, take refuge in the equally high but more relaxing scenery of the Trentino.

Despite common belief, Milan is not just an enormous city strangled by traffic and smog where all the contradictions of a consumer civilization are to be found. To those who know how to appreciate it, the capital of Lombardy can offer the unusual poetry of the Navigli (canals), the brio of the "Senigallia" (flea market), and the old-fashioned romanticism of Brera.

The effervescence of the city is obvious to anyone who walks along the central streets or who stops off in Piazza del Duomo to watch the multicolored, heterogeneous crowd bustling by. A walk along the elegant Via della Spiga or Via Montenapoleone, will confirm the snobbish love for beautiful things that has made Milan the center of refined Italian fashion, which is envied by everyone. Getting to know the real Milanese, means taking a walk in the Galleria at aperitif-time, or sipping a coffee on the panoramic terrace of the Rinascente department store. Then enjoy the unexpected peace of the streets of old Milan or, near Sant'Ambrogio, the domain of antique dealers. In Sant'Ambrogio the annual fair of "O bei O bei" is held on December 7, the patron saint's feast day, and on the same day the lyrical season begins at the Scala, the world's most famous opera house, given the dedication of the musicians and singers and the perfection of its performances.

Italy is all of this and still more. Through 3000 years of history, the nation has served as a center for art and human events and the culture of the Western world. While conscious of the wealth of their past, the Italian people have kept their eternally youthful spirit and their love for life. Discrediting the clichés that once described it as a sluggish and indifferent nation, modern Italy is an important economic power and very much a presence on the international scene.

Pride in the Past: Confidence in the Future

To speak of Italian cities is to speak of art, history, culture, and life in a delicate equilibrium that is constantly renewed. Each city sums up the charm of the past through its buildings and monuments and the perpetual motion of everyday life. The different styles of the various epochs can be seen in the architectural forms of every building or monument, street or square. But history is not only to be found in architecture – the histories of cities are always written by their inhabitants. Generous or genial, reserved or spontaneous, the people are what make each city unique.

32 top *The Upper Church of St. Francis has dominated Assisi since its consecration in 1253. The eight years that were required to restore this Gothic masterpiece are indicative of its complexity.*

32 bottom *Surrounded by a canal in the center of Padua, the Prato della Valle contains a number of statues of famous citizens.*

33 *The Basilica of San Vitale in Ravenna is one of the purest creations of paleo-Christian art in Italy. The interior is decorated with splendid Byzantine mosaics of scenes taken from the Old Testament and the processions of Emperor Justinian and Empress Theodora.*

Rome: A Monument unto Itself

34-35 *The Trevi Fountain has reacquired its original dazzling splendor and exerts an irresistible pull on tourists, some of whom undoubtedly nostalgically recall* la dolce vita *of a world that no longer exists.*

35 top *Bernini designed the statues of angels that embellish Sant'Angelo bridge.*

35 bottom *The statues of the Dioscuri stand at the center of the Piazza del Quirinale on the highest of the seven hills of Rome.*

36-37 *The bright light of the Roman sky is reflected in the spectacular and triumphant architecture of the Piazza di Spagna, which is dominated by the Trinità dei Monti Church.*

38-39 *Rising above the stalls in Piazza Campo de' Fiori is the monument to Giordano Bruno, who in 1600 was burned at the stake here for heresy.*

40 *Inside the church of San Pietro in Vincoli is a mausoleum which Pope Julius II commissioned Michelangelo to build for him. The tomb was never completed. Of the statues the artist designed and sculpted for it, only is the statue of Moses remains today. Vasari, an artist and biographer of the period, wrote that no other sculpture, either past or future, would ever equal it.*

41 *Heart of the Catholic world and tangible emblem of Christianity, St. Peter's Basilica contains inestimable art treasures, including Michelangelo's* Pietà. *The statue of the Virgin holding Christ expresses grief and regret with a touching sensitivity. A subtle sense of movement pervades the composition.*

42-43, 43 top *St. Peter's Basilica only truly reveals its full grandeur when it is packed with worshippers, in this case on the occasion of the coronation of Pope Benedict XVI, on 24 April 2005.*

43 bottom *Under the Pope's guidance, representatives of the Diocese of Rome line up in the enormous interior of the Basilica, which is so large and complex that it took three centuries to complete.*

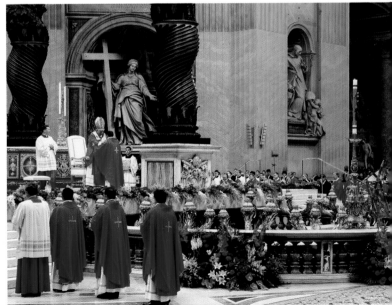

43

44-45 *Considered the very symbol of the eternity of Rome, the Colosseum was inaugurated by Emperor Titus in A.D. 80, after eight years of work. The huge amphitheater was destined for contests between gladiators and wild beasts.*

45 top left *The Roman Forum, a spectacular complex of temples, basilicas and votive monuments, was the heart of public life in ancient Rome. From the 17th century on, the archeology of the site has gradually been revealed.*

45 bottom *The Arch of Constantine, one of the best preserved of all Roman arches, was built near the Colosseum to celebrate Emperor Constantine's victory over Maxentius.*

45 right *The large exedra of Trajan's Market, dating from the first century A.D., consists of two stories of workshops surmounted by a splendid panoramic terrace.*

Cosmopolitan Milan

Proud of its status as Italy's principal commercial center in Milan has gained particular recognition in the field of international high fashion. The stock exchange here is the most important in the country, and its location is a sign of the leading position Milan holds in Italian industry. Busy, sometimes frenetic, Milan is among the most dynamic of European cities.

46 left Even the clanging electric trams must fight their way through the many difficulties of Milanese traffic.

46 top right Milan is not a city of skyscrapers. Indeed, the cathedral, in the background, is always visible from the upper floors of the buildings.

46 bottom right The Galleria is the site of some of the city's most elegant restaurants and is a traditional meeting place of the Milanese.

47 Built between 1865 and 1877, the Galleria Vittorio Emanuele II connects Piazza del Duomo and Piazza della Scala. Elegant metallic structures support the glass vaults which cast a luminous light on multicolored mosaics on the floor of the Galleria.

48-49 The cathedral is once more resplendent with its original whiteness restored, highlighting a phantasmagorical forest of 135 Gothic spires.

Turin: the Lady

The visitor who arrives in Turin for the first time realizes that he is in a setting very different from that of other Italian cities. This sensation is due to the dignified and slightly outmoded appearance of the layout of the city's street and squares, a heritage dating from Roman times. Despite the city's arduous postindustrial conversion that followed the crises of the Eighties and Nineties, the Piedmontese capital is still associated with its image as the old capital of the Kingdom of Italy

and as a prestigious cultural center. Turin's beauty is further enhanced by its position on the banks of the Po, at the foot of hills overlooked by the Alps. The city was selected by the International Olympic Committee, to be the venue for the 2006 Winter Olympics.

50 and 51 Despite Turin's reputation as a not very varied city, it actually boasts an array of eclectic architecture and inspired incongruities, including the Mole Antonelliana, above, which was built as a synagogue at the end of the 19th century and which is now a museum; the "extreme Baroque" of the lantern of Guarino Guarini's 16th-century church of San Lorenzo; and Palazzo Madama, which is a unique sort of Neoclassical wing added to a medieval castle which has parts dating back to Roman times.

Venice: Labyrinth of Water

Together with Florence and Rome, Venice, the ancient Queen of the Adriatic, holds a place as one of the major centers of Italian art. The city's magnificent palaces reveal the influence of Oriental, Italian Baroque and Renaissance styles. Since Venice is built on an archipelago of more than 100 small islands, the principal thoroughfares of the city consist of innumerable canals which are usually crowded with boats of all sorts. Among these, the slender gondola remains unique. To discover the most hidden corners of the city, walk down the narrow, winding lanes which suddenly open onto *campielli*, the settings for the most authentic Venetian life.

52 left top *When the soft, golden light of the setting sun envelops its cupolas, St. Mark's Basilica is a magical place.*

52 center left *The Rialto Bridge, the largest and best-known bridge in Venice, was built in 1592. It is in the heart of one of the city's best shopping areas.*

52 bottom left *Each year, the Vogalonga, along with the Regata Storica and the Festa del Redentore, commemorate the maritime traditions of the old Venetian Republic.*

52 center *The Ca' d'Oro (the Golden House) on the Grand Canal is a masterpiece of Venetian Gothic architecture. Its name comes from the fact that it was once covered in gold.*

52 right *The Lion of St. Mark is the symbol of the city; high atop its column it welcomes visitors as they disembark in St. Mark's Square.*

53 *The multicolored marble façade and the skillful design of the walls and supporting arches give an impression of extreme lightness to the Doge's Palace.*

54-55 *Two Venetians in costume strike a pose with the island of San Giorgio in the background.*

56 top *The richly decorated rooms inside the Doge's Palace feature carved ceilings adorned with friezes and painted panels.*

56 bottom *Now famous for its chic atmosphere, the Café Florian was the setting for patriotic conspiracies during the Austrian occupation.*

57 *At the top of the clock tower in St. Mark's Square, the famous animated statues of the two Moors have been striking the hours every day since 1497.*

Verona: City of the Scaligeri

The major attraction of Verona, one of the most significant cities of art in northern Italy, is the Arena, one of the best-preserved of all Roman amphitheaters. Built in the first century A.D., this superb monument regains its historic splendor during the summer opera season. Because of the grandeur of the setting, Giuseppe Verdi's *Aida* is a particular favorite.

Magnificent Florence

On the border of the upper and lower Arno Valley, enclosed by a circle of hills covered with olive trees, pines and cypresses, is Florence, the cradle of the Italian language and the city where Dante began writing. The history of Florence is closely connected with that of the Medici family, the benefactors of some of the most illustrious Renaissance artists. Leonardo, Michelangelo and Botticelli made Florence the stronghold of ideal beauty. Lorenzo de' Medici, known as the Magnificent, was himself a talented poet as well as a generous patron of the arts. It is no wonder, given such an illustrious background, that Florence has made a great contribution to Italian civilization and is still an important cultural center with a unique historical character.

60 top left *From Piazzale Michelangelo a panoramic view of the city is divided in two by the Arno River.*

60 bottom left *The Boboli Gardens in the grounds of Palazzo Pitti displays the dramatic landscaping typical of gardens designed in Italy in the second half of the 16th century.*

60 right *The Church of Santa Maria Novella is a hybrid of two styles. The lower half was completed in the Gothic period and the upper half was designed by Leon Battista Alberti 100 years later.*

61 *Giotto's campanile and Brunelleschi's immense Cathedral dome tower over the red roofs of the city.*

62-63 *Ponte Vecchio is lined on both sides by rows of goldsmith's and jeweler's shops.*

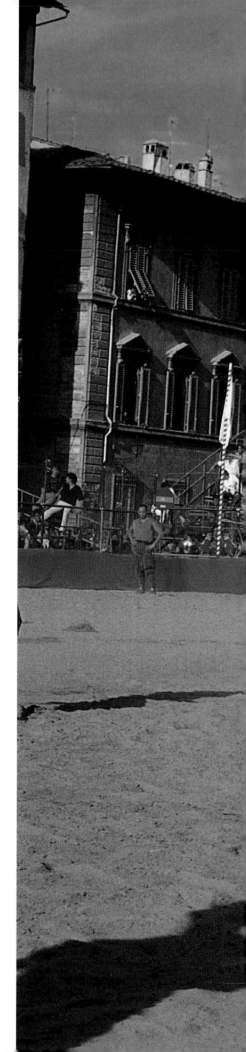

64 top *The Galleria dell'Accademia is famous for its sculptures by Michelangelo: the Palestrina Pietà, St. Matthew, the four unfinished Slaves originally designed for the tomb of Pope Julius II in Rome, and the famous David, a copy of which can be seen in Piazza della Signoria.*

64 center and bottom *Masterpieces of Italian painting from all periods are housed in the Uffizi, the single most important gallery for Italian art in the world. Valuable works from other European countries can be seen here, as well.*

64-65 *On the first Sunday in May and on June 24, football matches are held in the Piazza Santa Croce. The contests, which date back to the 16th century, are spectacular and rather violent.*

Siena: Reflection of Another Age

66 Siena's cathedral, completed at the end of the 13th century was intended to have been far larger, with the existing part forming the transept of the greater structure. However, the Black Death interrupted work in 1348 and the cathedral was never finished.

66-67 Visiting the center of Siena is like traveling back in time. Indeed, the appearance of the Piazza del Campo, dominated by the Mangia Tower (1348), has changed little since medieval days.

68 and 68-69 *Each year on 2 July and 16 August, a famous horse race called the Palio takes place in Siena's Piazza del Campo. The race is preceded by a procession in costume in which all the* contrade, *or city quarters, take part. The origin of this tradition dates back to the 14th century when, on the second day of July, a Medici soldier shot at an effigy of the Madonna. To make up for this sacrilege, a church was built and the Palio was organized.*

Naples:
the Taste of Surprise

"See Naples and die" is well-known saying, and in fact it would be difficult to find another city with an equally enchanting location and atmosphere. Overlooking a wide gulf, its houses built on the surrounding hills with Vesuvius on guard in the background, Naples offers one of the most spectacular panoramas in the Mediterranean. While the misery and heroism of Naples has been so well captured in the films of De Sica and Totò, the true soul of the city is to be found

in the busy neighborhoods that surround the city's historic center. Here, behind the crumbling façades and closed doors in front of which boys play football, are incredibly beautiful courtyards and staircases.

70-71 and 71 left The history of each of Naples' conquerors and governors is tied up with that of the Castel dell'Ovo, which was built on Roman foundations and repeatedly remodeled up until the 16th century.

71 right Visitors to Naples may experience a strange sense of déjà vu in the Galleria Umberto I (1884), as the general layout of the arcade and its roof were inspired by Milan's Galleria Vittorio Emanuele II (1867). However, the impression of refined grandeur is identical in both.

Pompeii and Paestum: Traces of the Past

Founded at the foot of Vesuvius by the Oscans during Roman times, Pompeii was a flourishing city when Vesuvius erupted during the night of August 24th in A.D. 79. The town was literally covered with a shower of red-hot lava. Preserved by the volcanic ash, the city now provides us with a complete example of the layout of towns during the Roman Empire. The city of Paestum had a different destiny.

It was founded in the 7th century B.C. by Greek colonists and given the name of Posidonia before being buried by time and forgotten by man. Until the 18th century, when a number of adventurous foreign travelers were attracted by the romanticism of the ruins, Paestum remained hidden and ignored amid the marshes and forests that held its treasures almost intact.

72 left The Stabian Way passes the Great Theatre and the Odeion, heading straight for the slopes of Vesuvius, which buried the town with its eruption in A.D. 79.

72 top right and bottom The paintings Pompeii celebrate all aspects of Roman life, from the sacred (top, Dionysian rite) to the secular (bottom, silverware).

73 As Pompeii became a flourishing commercial center, its houses were modified and turned into elegant dwellings.

74-75 *A triumph of the Doric order, Paestum offers views full of that antique charm that so captivated the 19th-century Romantics. In this view, the north portico of the "Basilica" (Temple of Hera) frames the fluted columns of the Temple of Poseidon (that was actually also consecrated to Hera) in the background.*

75 top *The temple of Neptune is one of the most beautiful and best-preserved Doric structures remaining at Paestum.*

75 bottom *The temple of Ceres was dedicated to the goddess Athena and in the Middle Ages it was converted into a church.*

Palermo: Crossroads of Cultures

The urban layout of Palermo sums up Sicily's many contradictory characteristics. The sharp contrasts between the old and new parts of Palermo reveal both the ancient influences and the aspirations of a modern metropolis. Founded by the Phoenicians, the city was conquered by the Romans around 250 B.C. Later, after the Arabs defeated the Byzantines, Palermo experienced a period of great prosperity which lasted until the arrival of the Normans. The successive Angevin, Aragonese and Spanish periods left the city with Gothic remains and Baroque features while deeply influencing the character of the population. The beauty of Palermo is to be found in the composite character of its culture and monuments.

76 top left In the streets of the old center, the voices of the street vendors blend in with the confusion of the passers-by.

76 bottom left Popular shows featuring the pupi, or marionettes, tell the ancient legends of Norman heroes.

76 center The church of San Giovanni, built by Roger II in 1132, is one of the most characteristic monuments of Norman Palermo, despite the fact that its red cupolas give it an Oriental appearance.

76 right Two slender towers flank the apse of the cathedral, which dates from 1158.

77 The cathedral, a composite of different architectural styles, overlooks a square filled with greenery. Inside the church are the relics of Santa Rosalia, the patron saint of the city.

Agrigento, Selinunte, Segesta: Where Nature and History Complement One Another

A journey through the oldest remains of ancient Sicily has always been a return to the natural elements. Builders in the classical world knew the intimate secrets of the island and how to use the subtle play of light and color in the landscape to their greatest advantage. The mystical bond which united the Greek colonies to the Divine presence was so strongly felt that each city boasted the protection of a god or a supernatural hero. Even today this bond can still be felt by the more attentive visitor, who will sense the mystery of proportion among the ancient stones. The theaters and temples of Selinunte, Agrigento and Segesta represent a balance between architecture and the natural landscape which has yet to be equaled.

78 top left *A group of four columns is all that remains of the temple of Castor and Pollux.*

78 top right and 78-79 *The largest temple at Selinunte is Temple C, with 17 columns along the sides and 6 columns along the front.*

78 bottom right *In the valley of the temples at Agrigento, a number of sacred buildings date from the Greek epoch. Of these, the best preserved is the Concordia Temple.*

80 left *Segesta was founded in the twelfth century BC and subsequently became a flourishing Greek colony. The Doric temple and Hellenistic theatre date back to this era.*

80-81 *The temple of Agrigento, dedicated to Hercules, dates from 520 B.C. Delimited by its rectangular frame of 38 columns, it is one of the largest and most spectacular of its kind.*

An Iridescent Fable

"That which the sea gives, the sea can take away" is an old fisherman's saying, The ancient legends of Scylla and Charybidis and of the sorceress Circe bear witness to the contest between man and sea. When many still believed that the Mediterranean was the center of the world and there was nothing else beyond it, the desire for adventure and knowledge moved the spirit of the great navigators, pushing them to undertake voyages which demanded great fortitude and dedication. The history of the sea is not only told by the suffering of the fishermen who had to fight every day to scrape a living from it, but also by the riches and power some cities managed to acquire from maritime commerce.

82 top *The old fishing village of Positano is characterized by white houses scattered in picturesque disorder above a small cove on the Amalfi coast.*

82 bottom *On the rocky coast of the Gargano peninsula, known for its small coves hidden by pine trees, the town of Vieste stands on a steep promontory with beaches on either side.*

83 *Portofino, on the Riviera di Levante, has become a legendary jet-set resort that has nonetheless preserved the charm of an old fishing village.*

Liguria: Mountain Bow Drawn Across the Waves

The Ligurian Apennines and the Maritime Alps rise steeply from the Gulf of Genoa, leaving the province only a narrow coastal strip. Liguria is a kind of landscape model of the Mediterranean shore, divided into two zones with different characteristics. The coast to the east provides a sharp contrast between the mountains and the sea, while the Riviera di Ponente is generally less rugged.

84 top left *The village of Camogli retains much of its original character.*

84 right *Camogli boasts an ancient maritime tradition; it is said that the inhabitants of this village taught the art of seafaring to the whole of Europe.*

84 bottom *On the second Sunday in May, a feast called the Padellata takes place in which fresh fish is fried in huge pans.*

84-85 *The colorful port of Camogli dates from the 17th century.*

86-87 *The church of Santa Maria Assunta and the ruins of the Dragone castle stand on a rock promontory that dominates the port of Camogli.*

88-89 *Heavy seas beat against the harbor at Camogli.*

Cinque Terre:
The Relationship
Between Man and the Sea

Manarola and Vernazza are two of the five small villages known as the Cinque Terre which nestle at the western end of the Gulf of La Spezia. Until not very long ago, the only means of communication was by the sea, rail or a path which was at times dangerously exposed. Even today the autumnal high seas increased the sense of isolation in these precipitous places.

Island Jewels

Among Italy's smaller islands, Capri is a precious jewel anchored in an intensely blue sea. Though attracting tourists from all over the world, Capri has managed, on the whole, to preserve its natural beauty. The immense calcareous blocks which form the island rise out of a deep sea. Capri has a jagged and inaccessible coast, which sometimes forms steep cliffs with fantastic profiles or ones in which the waves have created dramatic niches and cavities. The most elaborate effects of erosion can be seen in the natural arches or in the romantic Blue Grotto, the sea cave famous for the way light refracts to give it an intense turquoise color.

Although it is not crowded, the nearby island of Ponza has no cause to be jealous of its more famous neighbor. Here, too, there is the same jagged coastline, crowned by numerous cliffs wich highlight a landscape still wild and exciting. The somber and intense color of Ponza's rock is similar to the volcanic landscape of the Sicilian island of Lampedusa, the main island in the Pelagian group. White villages stand out clearly in this lunar grayness, as do isolated dwellings surrounded by the meager vegetation to thrive – only broom manages to thrive, and its flowers add color in spring. The volcanic rock forms a sharp contrast with the surrounding deep-blue crystalline waters. The primordial beauty of the coast has been preserved despite the summer assault of tourists.

92 top Capri's famous rock formations rise from the depths of the clear blue sea.

92 center The island of Ponza has a rugged coastline composed of high walls of multicolored volcanic rock.

92 bottom The adventures of Odysseus are recalled in Italy's romantic seascapes.

93 The island of Lampedusa, which extends arid and flat over an area of about 7.7 square miles (20 sq. kilometers), is the most southerly part of Italy.

94-95 Once a penal colony, the island of Capraia in the Tuscan Archipelago is now a nature park.

The Kingdom of Circe

96 top and bottom and 96-97 *Sheer rocky coasts with villages nestling on the top, coves, beaches, cliffs and sea grottoes, all contained in an area of less than 8 sq. miles (20.7 sq. kilometers): this is the magic of Ponza, an island that seems to be a world unto itself, suspended between Homeric memories and the sunny Mediterranean reality.*

Wild Beauty Overlooking the Sea

Some of Italy's most rugged coastline comes to an end amid the waves of the Gulf of Salerno and along the coasts of the splendid Pontine Island where the coastline exhibits its unusual eroded forms. Hidden between the many spurs of rock are wild ravines and tiny coves used by the fishermen to beach their boats. On the rocks are clumps of evergreen plants and hedges of prickly pears. A large number of terraces, held up by high walls and the patient toil of man, are planted with olives, vines, and oranges, each with its particular shade of green. In this setting, the fishermen's houses, with their warm, sunny colors, fit in harmoniously.

98 The precipitous rocks, steep crags, and deep gorges of the Amalfi Coast have earned it universal fame.

99 Atrani, entirely surrounded by the sea and rocky precipices, has a glorious past, for along with adjoining Amalfi, it was one of the earliest Italian maritime republics, predating even that of Venice.

100-101 Nestled between the mountains and the sea, Amalfi projects an image of lively and evocative beauty.

Sardinia: Island of Contrasts

102-103 *In the small island of Budelli, nature has skillfully mixed its colors: green waters, pink beaches, and tenacious vegetation give this coastline and unparalleled charm.*

104-105 *Mediterranean scrub and granite reign supreme in the folds of Cape Falcone, the northwestern tip of Sardinia.*

Sardinia's coastal landscape displays an amazing variety of forms as a result of the water's erosive force. At the edge of the sea, the waves batter the rock; in the inlets, the coast reveals the entire range of its colors, from somber to bright. High mountains fall steeply into waters whose colors range from green to turquoise, and the imposing granitic formations slope down more gently, constantly modeled by the action of the waves.

106-107 *Cape Testa, at the north of the island, is one of Sardinia's most interesting natural areas.*

107 top *The rugged spurs of the northern coast of the island of La Maddalena extend into the sea.*

107 left *Hollowed by the action of sea and wind, the rocks of the Sardinian coast reflect the variety of the island's forms and colors.*

107 center *The color of the sea at Stintino seems even more extraordinary because of the contrast with the white beach.*

107 bottom *With variations in light and weather, the sea around Sardinia constantly takes on new shades and a different character.*

The Mountains: Enormous Sentinels

The imposing Alpine arc, guardian of northern Italy, contains Europe's highest peaks and constitutes one of the most important geographical features of the country. Soaring, windswept summits, dazzling white glaciers, desolate stretches of morainic scree, rugged, rocky or verdant valleys, raging torrents and peaceful lakes glittering like gems form a magnificent landscape. But man has left his imprint. Path signs, shepherds' huts, and chapels remind us of the hard work and dedication of the mountain people who continue to pass on their archaic traditions. For these people, the Alps are much more than a training ground for sports.

108-109 *The Monte Rosa massif is tinged with delicate shades of color at dawn and sunset. However, its name is not a poetic reference to these magnificent pinkish hues, but actually derives from the Celtic word* ros, *meaning ice.*

The Alps: Guardians of Italy

110 top *Les Grandes Jorasses form part of the Mont Blanc massif.*

110 bottom *Mont Blanc reaches a height of 15,780 ft. (4810 meters.)*

110-111 *The distinctive pyramid of the Matterhorn towers over the surrounding peaks.*

112-113 *The Dente del Gigante is one of the most difficult summits of the Mont Blanc massif.*

114-115 *The Alps offer striking panoramas of peaks and glaciers.*

116 *The Torri del Vaiolet is part of Dolomite range's Catinaccio Group.*

117 *The Brenta Dolomites, to the west of the River Adige, have a rich mountaineering history which began in about 1880.*

118-119 *The Sella group towers over the four surrounding valleys of Ladine like an immense monolith.*

The high rock walls and craggy summits of the Dolomites resemble the fanciful ruins of immense castles. Unlike the granitic Alpine ranges, the large calcareous masses of the Dolomite peaks are distinct and separate from each other, forming clearly defined groups. The range has always been a challenge to mountaineers, who must use special climbing techniques to scale the peaks. The deep pink of the dolomitic rock contrasts dramatically with the green forests and pastures which slope down to form the valley, studded here and there with small lakes. The flora of the Pale Mountains is among the richest in the entire Alpine arc, and is best represented by the yellow Rhaetian poppy.

120-121 *The Sella Massif consists of a single block of rock which can be reached only after crossing meadows, woods, screes, and rock faces. The Sella group rises from a vast plateau from which also emerges the peak of Piz Boé.*

121 top left *Besides climbers and hikers, the Dolomites have inspired writers, painters, directors and scriptwriters. The beauty of these mountains has been exploited in many famous films, including fantasy and action stories.*

121 top right *The towering, rugged Brenta Massif comprises some of the most beautiful peaks of the Dolomites. The photograph shows the southern part of the chain, which culminates in the 10,410-ft. (3173 m) Cima Tosa.*

121 bottom *The Rozes peak in the Tofane group dominates the basin of Cortina d'Ampezzo.*

Memories of
Life's Ancient Rhythms:
Val Badia

The Val Badia is inhabited by a minority of Ladins who continue to speak a dialect derived from Latin. The costumes and customs of the artisans and farmers of this ethnic group have survived intact through the years. Local settlements known as *vilas*, hamlets consisting of between six and twenty houses, still survive in this valley.

122-123 *The natural beauty of Val Badia offers breathtaking views long admired by tourists.*

123 *The residents of Val Badia gather each year for a precession in honor of the Sacred Heart of Jesus.*

The Sibylline Mountains

The Sibylline Mountains conjure up memories of ancient rites and mysterious legends. According to legend, Sibyl's cavern was located among these heights, where an enchanted world filled with marrelous treasures opened up at the end of a deep grotto. Today these mountains, crisscrossed by deep gorges and steep gullies, still provide a habitat for wolves and wildcats, golden eagles and peregrine falcons. The slopes are sometimes softened by a blanket of snow in winter; in spring the meadow are covered with wildflowers. Nestled in a valley or perched on an isolated mountain crest, these tiny villages still hand down all the marvels of a world which has changed very little. Even today, an encounter with fairies seems more than just a figment of the imagination.

124-125 The old hamlet of Castelluccio, standing out against the snowy mass of Mt. Vettore, is the highest in the Sibylline Mountains.

In the Mouth of the Volcano

According to the myth, Vulcan was the lord of fire and metal forging. With the help of the Cyclops he worked in the hidden recesses of Mt. Etna. Recalling the ancient legend, Mt. Etna dominates the Sicilian landscape, offering views of unrivaled beauty. It is the largest volcano in Europe, with its central crater at a height of over 9845 ft. (3000 m). The precipitous Bove Valley cuts deep into the mountainside, and 250 craters formed by lateral eruptions scar its surface. Over the millennia, the volcano's activity has created a unique environment and has always challenged those who have stubbornly faced the continuous danger of eruptions to settle on its fertile slopes. There are other volcanoes on the islands; Stromboli has a single crater which is more or less in constant activity.

126 top *The imposing cone of Mt. Etna rises along Sicily's eastern coast.*

126 bottom *Nocturnal excursions to the Stromboli volcano are very popular with tourists who visit the island.*

127 *With a guide, the more adventurous may still climb up Mt. Etna until close to one of the many craters to witness the awsome sight of erupting lava.*

128 *The dome of St. Marks Basilica rises above the morning mists which linger over Venice's lagoon.*